ruth

A **SIMPLY BIBLE** STUDY

CARMEN BEASLEY

For Jesus,
my Redeemer.

For I know that my Redeemer lives,
and at the last he will stand upon the earth.
JOB 19:25

And for both my grandmas,
who suffered tragedy and trials without bitterness.

AS THE LORD LIVES,

I WILL REDEEM YOU.

RUTH 3:13

table of *contents*

RUTH | A **SIMPLY BIBLE** STUDY

INTRODUCTION

STUDY CONTENT

APPENDIX

welcome

A REDEMPTION STORY

THE LORD GRANT THAT
YOU MAY FIND REST...

RUTH 1:9

welcome to *ruth*

A REDEMPTION STORY

IN DAY TO DAY LIVING, TRAGEDY ABOUNDS. Today's local newspaper headlines feature the random murder of a beloved husband and father, the devastation of a global pandemic ravaging the world, and a sordid affair of unfaithfulness.

Part of me wonders why in the world I continue to read a newspaper or scroll through the day's news events online? It's depressing. Tomorrow's headlines will involve different names and circumstances, yet similar tragedy. Life is full of heartbreak. None of us live unscathed by it.

Beyond tragedy are the trials. Similar to tragedy, trials hit everyone and seemingly unfold like the waves of the ocean, rolling (or maybe crashing) in, day-after-unglamorous day. Welcome to the ordinary. The mundane. The disappointments. Broken dreams. The struggle bus. The world is seemingly full of people getting by on lemons without the sugar needed to turn them into lemonade. In the midst of ongoing tragedy and trials, it's no wonder that depression is sky-rocketing!

Finally, as if tragedy and trials are not enough, there is the big lie: *Everyone else's life is perfectly lovely.*

Hop on social media to see for yourself. View the smiles of friends, co-workers, and family. See the perfect teeth, the perfect marriage, the perfect kids, the perfect vacation, the perfect everything.

In our online celebrity culture, where social media portrays the lives of everyday, regular people and the lives of the rich and famous as both glamorous and beautiful, it's easy to feel marginalized, side-lined... and become bitter.

Generally speaking, the word *bitter* relates to the sense of taste. The Old Testament mentions bitter herbs (Exodus 12:8), bitter grapes (Deuteronomy 32:32), and bitter water, which comes by its bitterness either naturally ("Marah," Exodus 15:23) or because of a divine curse (Numbers 5:17). [1]

Figuratively speaking, bitterness often expresses pain or hopelessness. To be bitter can mean to be resentful. Even hateful. Something like carrying a chip on your shoulder.

Not only did God give us taste buds to help us experientially recognize bitterness, He utilizes this taste experience metaphorically and graciously warns us against the "roots of bitterness" that can spring up in our hearts:

> See to it that no one fails to obtain the grace of God; that no "root of bitterness" springs up and causes trouble, and by it many become defiled...
>
> **HEBREWS 12:15**

These roots lead to trouble. Yet, most of us don't even realize that roots of bitterness exist within our own hearts. That's the tricky thing about roots. They're buried, hidden deep. Roots exist underground where the light does not shine.

Never really thought of yourself as bitter? Then ask God to prick or shine His Holy Spirit light on your heart as you reflect on the following questions:

---

[1] Myers, A. C. (1987). **The Eerdmans Bible Dictionary** (p. 161). Grand Rapids, MI: Eerdmans.

- What's your reaction to a friend's happy social media post? Bitter or sweet?
- Is there a whiff of jealousy in your heart?
- Are you discontent in any way?
- Ever carried or currently carry a grudge?
- Are you experiencing difficulty in forgiving another?
- Do you have unhealthy go-to places for seeking comfort? Like food, alcohol, pornography, shopping, or lamely browsing the internet?
- Ever feel cynical, distrustful, resentful, or suspicious towards others (or God)?
- Do you feel a sense of hopelessness or an inability for change?
- Ever wonder if God see you, hears you, or loves you?
- Have you ever asked, "Does God care?"

If you answered "yes" to any one of these questions, bitterness could be lurking in the shadows. Perhaps down deep lies a wound. Wounds hurt. And these tender places are where roots of bitterness are most likely to sprout and hide. This remains especially true if we turn to other things in order to placate the hurt. Roots are stubborn things. Outwardly, all can appear well, but inwardly lurks trouble.

So, in the midst of living in this fallen world with its tragedy, trials, and lies, how does one keep from bitterness?

WELCOME TO THE REMARKABLE STORY OF RUTH.

This Old Testament biblical narrative begins with devastating tragedy, trials, and even a lie, but ends with good news of great joy. This is a redemption story. If you long for recovery, restoration, or revival, then this is for you.

Much hope can be gleaned from the characters of Ruth. In this study, we will look closely at the book's namesake: Ruth, a loyal and faithful Moabite widow; Naomi, Ruth's widowed and embittered mother-in-law who grieves the loss of her sons; Boaz, their generous and dynamic kinsman redeemer; and most of all, the God of the Bible, who proves steadfast in His love and mercy.

SO COME! Find the anecdote to bitterness in God's grace. Studying Ruth is an invitation similar to David's song:

> Oh, taste and see that the Lord is good!
> Blessed is the man who takes refuge in him!
>
> PSALM 34:8

Ruth did. As a foreign widow, she could have chosen bitterness. Rather, Ruth sought refuge in the Lord God Almighty and experienced His goodness.

So, whether hopeless or hopeful, whether experiencing tragedy or, like me, you only suffer from a tendency to be overcome by first-world problems and trials, may you know the blessing of God's refuge. May the God of the Bible encourage you through these noble and sometimes not-so-noble characters where loyalty, boldness, and generosity prosper. May the lies of "God doesn't care" be exchanged for the truth of God's steadfast love and faithfulness.

Tragedy, trials, and lies are found at the root of the gospel—the good news—story, but these are by no means the end of the story. I am so excited to begin this journey with you!

With much joy,

Carmen

PS—Connect with us and join our online community at **simplybiblestudy.com**, **Facebook: Simply Bible Study Group**, or **YouTube: Simply Bible Study.**

inductive study

AN INTRODUCTION TO **SIMPLY BIBLE**

WHY HAVE I FOUND FAVOR IN
YOUR EYES, THAT YOU SHOULD
TAKE NOTICE OF ME, SINCE I
AM A FOREIGNER?

RUTH 2:10

inductive bible study

AN INTRODUCTION TO **SIMPLY BIBLE**

AS A LITTLE GIRL, I ADORED COLORING BOOKS. Smooth, crisp white pages displayed bold black lines of perfectly-drawn figures and characters. The spaces patiently awaited color. Fondly, I remember the joy of opening a new pack of crayons. The waxy smell and the neat little rows of pointed tips colorfully peeked out and tantalized me as if to say, "Try to choose just one!" Creativity awaited. Or so I thought.

When my four children were small, a friend of a friend encouraged me to forgo purchasing coloring books for them. My initial reaction was one of horror. "What? Coloring books are fun! That would be forgoing fun! Plain paper? How boring!" Okay, granted... my reaction was a little melodramatic, but I do remember thinking these thoughts.

Instead, this friend insisted that providing children with blank sheets of paper was the way to spur creativity. I could see the wisdom. Not to mention, a ream of paper was way cheaper than four new coloring books... and so, I gave it a try. Does this mean I never gave my children coloring books? No! My children certainly enjoyed a few here and there. However, I admit that these books never seemed to offer my children the same kind of joy that coloring books had offered me. And so, for the most part, my children simply grew up with lots of plain white paper and a variety of colorful pencils, crayons, and markers.

PLAIN, WHITE PAPER IT WAS. What happened? My kids learned to draw. Not just little stick figures in the middle of the page, but they learned to tell a story using a piece of paper. Masterpieces. (So this mom deems them.)

Now, I'm sure no one ever saved one of my coloring book pages. Oh, for sure! Sometimes one landed on Grandma's refrigerator. However, right now, in my basement, there remain binders of pictures that my budding artists created over twenty years ago.

Why? These pictures were windows into their little souls and minds. For example, if God was not present in a Bible story, my son would draw a big eye in the sky. In his little five-year-old heart, he understood that God could see him. Had I handed my children coloring book pages where they filled in the blanks, I would never have experienced windows like this into their hearts and minds.

Their works of art tell stories. And I treasure them in my heart.

THIS IS THE GIST OF **SIMPLY BIBLE**. These guides provide a "blank page" for reading and directly engaging with God and His Word. Rather than fill-in-the-blank questions, SIMPLY BIBLE offers space to be curious and ask your own questions. You will learn to observe, understand, and apply. Don't get me wrong: just like coloring books, traditional Bible studies have their place. Without them, I wouldn't be the Bible student that I am today. And yet, I am rather fond of this SIMPLY BIBLE series. With gentle direction, these books allow quiet spaces for listening to and knowing God, relating with Him by sharing in His story: *simply the Bible.*

Since its inception, I've known the joy and privilege of watching others seek God through SIMPLY BIBLE. I've watched these Bible study journals become windows into hearts, souls, and minds growing with God. These workbooks tell personal stories. And although the stories are often much too private for me to observe closely, I treasure each one in my heart. If I could, I'd pile them up in my basement. Perhaps it's cheesy, but in some tender way, they all pile up in the "basement in my heart."

Finally, I want to thank Melissa Trew. SIMPLY BIBLE would not be the same without her. As a gifted designer, she takes ordinary ideas and transforms them into extraordinarily beautiful workbooks. Coffee-table-worthy. Melissa, I am eternally grateful. Thank you.

SO WELCOME TO **SIMPLY BIBLE**! The rest of the introduction provides step-by-step guidance on getting started with the inductive Bible study method. You'll find everything you need to know to engage directly with God and His Word. Please read these sections before beginning the study.

MY DAUGHTER, SHOULD I NOT
SEEK REST FOR YOU, THAT IT
MAY BE WELL WITH YOU?

RUTH 3:1

simply bible

AN INDUCTIVE BIBLE STUDY

After her first study, a friend described SIMPLY BIBLE as "leaving behind her paint-by-numbers set for a blank canvas." Whether painting, drawing, or digging into God's Word, using a blank canvas can be a little intimidating. It takes practice! Just as artists learn a particular method and handle special tools to create a masterpiece, so do Bible study students.

The methodology utilized within SIMPLY BIBLE is known as *inductive study*. This method is used by Bible scholars, pastors, teachers, and students of all levels, and can easily be completed using a Bible and plain notebook. Frankly, the SIMPLY BIBLE workbooks are not necessary for inductive study. However, most readers agree that these user-friendly guides simplify and ease the study process by providing everything needed in one place via an easy-to-follow, logical format.

The inductive method involves three basic steps that often overlap with one another:

(1) Observe
(2) Interpret
(3) Apply

This three-step format helps to paint a more thorough understanding of God's Word.

On the following pages, you will find A QUICK-START GUIDE TO **SIMPLY BIBLE**. Bookmark and use this as needed. The quick-start guide is followed by a more thorough explanation of the format and basic study tools. Take time to get a feel for each step. Read the examples. And then, dig in!

getting *started*

A QUICK-START GUIDE

getting *started*

A QUICK-START GUIDE

READ	OBSERVE	INTERPRET
Read the passage. Try some or all of these ideas to help you read carefully. (Highlighters and colored pencils are fun here!)	As you read, write down your observations in this column. Simply notice what the Scripture *says*. This is your place for notes. Ideas include:	In this column, record what the passage *means*.
• Read the passage in a different version.	• Ask questions of the text, like "who, what, when, where, or how."	One way to interpret is to answer any questions asked during observation. Try to first answer these *without* the aid of other helps. Allow Scripture to explain Scripture. It often does.
• Read it out loud.	• Jot down key items: people, places, things. Mark places on a map.	If the answers are not intuitive or easily found near the passage, other tools are available. Use boxes A, B, and C to identify a key word, define it, and look up a cross reference. This extra research will shed light on the meaning.
• Underline, circle, box, or highlight repeated words, unfamiliar words, or anything that pricks your heart or catches your attention.	• Ask, "What does this passage say about God? Jesus? Holy Spirit?"	
• Listen to the passage while running errands.	• Note what took place before and after this passage.	IMPORTANT: *Seek to understand what the Scripture meant to the original author of Ruth and his original readers or hearers. Try to see and understand the world through the eyes of the Jewish people living in the ancient Near East culture.*
• Doodle or write out a verse in your workbook or a journaling Bible.	• Ponder.	
	• Ask God if there is anything else He'd like you to notice.	

PLEASE NOTE: The following boxes (labeled A, B, and C) are interpretation tools. These are meant to be used in unison with the "Interpret" column on the previous page to aid in interpreting Scripture. Most students find it helpful to complete these before interpreting. Consider this your toolbox. Find what's most helpful for you.

A KEY WORDS	**B** DEFINITIONS	**C** CROSS REFERENCES
When you notice a word that is repeated multiple times, unfamiliar, or interesting to you in any other way, record it here.	Record definitions of your key words. You can find the appropriate definitions by using: • a Bible concordance (defines words according to the original language) • a Bible dictionary • another translation	Note cross references. This is a solid way to allow Scripture to interpret Scripture. If your Bible does not include cross references, they can be found easily using web-based Bible resources.

Bible study tools like those listed above can be found by visiting the following websites:

blueletterbible.org   **biblegateway.com**   **biblehub.com**
stepbible.com   **logos.com**

MAIN POINTS	APPLY
Summarize the main point(s) or note any themes you encountered in the passage.	Apply God's Word specifically to your own life. Application is personal. God may teach, correct, rebuke, or train. He is always equipping. (II Tim. 3:16-17) Record what the passage means to you.

PRAY

Write a short prayer here. When we take time to write something down, that message becomes more etched on our heart. Take a moment to simply be with God. He is why we study. Savor. Know. Praise. Confess. Thank. Ask. Love. Then carry a nugget of His Word in your heart to ponder and proclaim throughout your day.

MAY YOU BE BLESSED BY
THE LORD, MY DAUGHTER.

RUTH 3:10

step by *step*

UNPACKING THE INDUCTIVE METHOD

step by *step*

UNPACKING THE INDUCTIVE METHOD

STEPS 1 & 2: READ AND OBSERVE | *See what the Bible **says**.*

The first step of Bible study is to observe God's Word.

In our hurried, scurried pace of life, we read too fast, often plowing through the words without taking time to ponder and think about what we're reading. *Observation* helps us to slow down and take notice in order to see. In this first step, we answer, "What does the Bible *say?*"

Have you ever stopped to truly examine and enjoy a piece of art? Artists develop an amazing knack or ability to capture a particular scene, whether real or imagined, onto a blank canvas. How? Artists specialize in observing details: setting, color, texture, time, characters, lighting, movement... The list of details is nearly limitless.

We can, too.

When my children were younger, blank sketch books and new drawing pencils equaled a special treat. With fresh, new artist tools in hand and a sunny day, my little ones and I would traipse excitedly through a park. Before pulling out a pencil to begin creating, we needed to find the right observation spot for observing. (I highly recommend that for Bible study, too!)

To observe means "to see, watch, notice, or regard with attention, especially so as to see or learn something." [1] *Especially so as to see or learn something.*

---

[1] **observe**. Dictionary.com. *Dictionary.com Unabridged.* Random House, Inc. http://www.dictionary.com/browse/observe (accessed: March 16, 2018).

And so, my children and I would notice things. Lots of things… the different types of leaves, flowers, plants, grass, insects, animals, and more. Once engaged in observing, details would begin to arise! How fun to zero in and observe the ladybug crawling along the blade of grass or the spots that adorn a toad sunning on the sidewalk or the veins that run throughout a maple leaf. There's so much to see!

Observation implies being curious. Noticing details. Asking questions.

Kids do this naturally. We can too. Be curious with God's Word. Scripture is full of details to notice and numerous questions to ask. When we slow down and take time to "smell the roses" within Scripture, we see and learn.

If you don't relate to art or being a kid again, then consider detective work. Inductive study is much like detective work. Detectives are trained to observe and notice details. They exude curiosity and examine cases by asking questions: who, what, when, where, how, and why.

Like detectives, we use observation skills too. Intuitively, without even thinking about it, we observe and interpret life around us.

Consider a family member or roommate. Using simple observation, we discern whether a loved one comes home happy, sad, or mad. After all, there's a huge difference between walking through the door with a smile or a frown. Singing a tune versus grumbling. Dancing versus slamming doors. We notice the "signs." And because we care, we ask questions. Inquisitive minds want to know, "What's up?" This leads to more questions: "Really? How? Why? Where? When? Who? Are you okay?" You get the picture.

Detective work transfers to reading and understanding God's Word. Observation means we read, study, and ask questions of the text. We look to see, "What does the Scripture say?" If short on time, we simply ask, "What does the Scripture say about who God is?"

As you read, pray and talk with God about His Word. Ask Him to help you see. Ask Him questions about the text. Highlight verses that touch your heart. If anything is especially noteworthy to you, jot it down in the space labeled **Observe** in your workbook. (Keep in mind: the SIMPLY BIBLE framework is just a guide. You can choose to fill in as little or as much as you desire.)

The bottom line? Read. Read carefully. Observe at least one thing, particularly something about God Himself. This allows us to see Scripture more clearly. This first step is the most important one. The bulk of study time should be spent here.

STEP 3: INTERPRET | *Understand what the Bible* **means**.

After careful observation of a landscape, an artist sketches an interpretation of what he sees onto the canvas. Observation and interpretation go hand in hand. A circle is a circle. A square is a square. As closely as possible, the artist defines and places an image of what he observes onto the canvas. Careful observation leads to a life-like rendering such that the viewer will understand what the artist himself observed.

The same is true of the Bible. Observation and interpretation go hand in hand. Scripture will often interpret Scripture. As we carefully read and observe what the scripture says, we frequently understand and simultaneously interpret it's *meaning*. So within our daily study format, observation and interpretation are located side-by-side.

One simple way to understand the meaning of Scripture is to answer the questions we asked in the observation process: the who, what, where, when, how, and why. Try to answer these questions without the aid of study notes or other helps. Utilize scripture to interpret scripture. Often, the answer is readily available.

Other times, interpretation is not so easy. After all, the Bible was written in ancient times, spanning the course of over two thousand years, *by* a people and *to* a people of a culture that is utterly foreign to us.

Therefore, certain resources are handy. These tools can help us to place and understand Scripture in its original context in order to properly interpret. (Think of an artist using a ruler—a simple tool that helps to more accurately reproduce a scene. A ruler is not necessary, but is useful.)

Bible study tools can include:

- *Cross references:* Cross references allow us to use nearby or related passages to more accurately interpret Scripture.
- *Bible dictionaries or concordances:* These tools allow students to understand the meaning of a word in its original language.
- *Bible handbooks and commentaries:* Resources like these help us to verify our conclusions as well as provide historical or cultural context.

It's important to remember that Scripture, in its original context, had only one meaning. Not multiple meanings. And although our God can be mysterious in His ways, there are no mystical or hidden meanings within Scripture.

The author of Ruth wrote a specific message, at a specific time, and in a specific place, for a specific group of people. He meant what he said. For this study, we want to know what the author *meant* and how the Israelites *understood* his words. Although we may not always be able to determine the author's specific intent, that is our goal.

Interpretation implies understanding. Original meaning and context are important. Be reasonable. Compare.

Seek correct answers, but give yourself grace. A child's rendering of a ladybug on a blade of grass will not equate to Van Gogh's renderings, and yet, there is something wholly precious about the works of a child. Our renderings of Scripture won't ever equate to a Bible scholar's commentary. That is not our goal. Our goal is knowing God. Sometimes this involves taking tiny baby steps in His direction. Humility is necessary.

A, B, & C: TOOLS FOR INTERPRETATION

If the answers to our questions are not intuitive or easily found within the passage, tools are available to help us better understand. Our daily lesson format provides three boxes intended to support interpretation. Here, you'll find space to identify key words, define those key words, and record supporting verses (cross references). These are intended to help and guide you as you interpret Scripture. Consider this to be your interpretation toolbox. Use the tools however you find them to be helpful.

A. KEY WORDS | Did you notice that a word was repeated, seems important, is unfamiliar, or interests you in any way? Record it here.

B. DEFINITIONS | Use this box to record definitions of the words you listed.

• *Read the verse using a different translation or version of the Bible.* This can be a very simple way to define a word. For example, our practice lesson (on page **24**) notes the word *void* from Genesis 1:2. The ESV version says "void," while the NIV translates the Hebrew as "empty." [1]

• *Use a Bible concordance.* This book looks at words in their original language. I like the **Strong's Concordance**, which can also be found online.

    i. Going online? Try **Blue Letter Bible**, a free web-based concordance.

    ii. Once there, (referring to our practice lesson on page **24**) simply type "Genesis 1" into the *Search the Bible* box. Select the box called *Tools* next to Genesis 1:2, and a menu appears. Find and select the corresponding Strong's Concordance number for "void" (in this case: H922). You'll retrieve the Hebrew word, original definitions, and where else it is used in Scripture. It's fascinating! Make note of the definitions you find.

---

[1] *The Holy Bible*, New International Version. Zondervan Publishing House, 2011.

- *Try a Bible dictionary.* In order to define people or locate places, Bible dictionaries are handy resources.

    i. Online, try **Bible Gateway, Blue Letter Bible, Bible Hub, Step Bible,** or **Logos.**

    ii. There are also wonderful apps available for you to use, including **Bible Map.** This simple-to-use app automatically syncs Scripture with maps.

C. CROSS REFERENCES | Many Bibles offer cross references. This is a rock-solid way to allow Scripture to interpret Scripture. If your Bible does not include cross references (most journaling Bibles do not), no worries! Accessing cross references online is easy.

Still not sure?

Note your question and talk to God about it. Ponder. As we ponder Scripture, God often illuminates our understanding. Other times, He allows certain things to remain unanswered. His ways are sometimes beyond our ways and our understanding. Ultimately, we walk by faith.

Remember to share and discuss your questions with others at Bible study. Studying God's Word is meant to be done in community where we learn and grow together in knowing, understanding, and loving God.

WANT MORE? Our daily study format includes space for definitions and cross references. However, there are other Bible study resources available if you'd like to dig even deeper.

Bible commentaries are written by Biblical scholars. These books provide cultural and historical context while commenting on Scripture verse-by-verse.

Personally, I admire the dedication and genius of scholars who write commentaries. These dedicated people study for the glory of God. And yet, I recommend saving their wonderful resources as a last step. Why? Because commentaries are not a substitute for reading, understanding, and engaging with God's Word on your own. First seek to understand God's Word without a commentary. Then, if desired, utilize a commentary for double-checking your work.

Also, please note that commentaries are written according to various theological bents. It's helpful to compare. Know your sources. This is especially crucial if roaming the Internet. Please surf with discernment and great care. I can't emphasize this enough. Unfortunately, even commentaries found on popular Bible study sites are not always researched or written by trained Biblical scholars. If unsure, background-check the author's credentials. Bible degrees and scholastic training from accredited universities and institutions are important.

To find reliable Biblical commentaries, I recommend:

bestcommentary.com   **challies.com**

SUMMARIZE: Your daily framework offers space for you to summarize and identify the main point(s) of the Bible passage you've read. If reading a narrative, consider summarizing the plot. Understanding the main idea of a passage helps to ensure a correct interpretation before moving into application.

STEP 4: APPLY | *Put it all **together**.*

Here's the "So what? How will I think or act differently because of God's Word?" With the Holy Spirit's help, observation and interpretation lead us to better understand the meaning of a Bible passage. That's thrilling! Discovering a nugget of truth, a promise or a revelation about God Himself takes my breath away and inevitably leads me to praise and worship Him. There is no other book like the Bible:

> For the word of God is living and active,
> sharper than any two-edged sword,
> piercing to the division of soul and of spirit,
> of joints and of marrow, and discerning
> the thoughts and intentions of the heart.
>
> HEBREWS 4:12

The God of the Universe loves us and personally reveals Himself through His Living Word. When He does, it cuts in a good way. This prepares us to apply His Word to our everyday lives in order to *think* and *act* differently.

APPLICATION IS THE CREATIVE PART. Yes, the original author of Scripture had one meaning, but the personal applications of Scripture are many. This step is between you and God. If a specific verse, word, or idea strikes a chord in your heart, *slow down*. Take note. Ponder. Show God the discovery. This is the amazing process of God revealing Himself and His truths to you through His Word and the power of His Spirit.

God looks at our hearts. He sees, knows, and loves His sheep. And so, He may use His Word to teach, correct, rebuke, or train. He is always equipping (II Timothy 3:16-17). If you're willing, God will lead you to apply His Word specifically to your everyday life.

Application ideas include:
1. Worship God for who He is, according to a truth or promise discovered.
2. Thank Him for a lesson learned.
3. Note an example to follow.
4. Confess a sin revealed.
5. Pray a prayer noticed.
6. Obey, trust, and follow God's way, His command, His plan.
7. Memorize a verse.

Bottom line? Ask yourself, "How will I think or act differently because of what I've learned in God's Word?"

WRAPPING UP: PRAY | *Respond to a **Holy God**.*

Application implies a recognition of who God is. And so, when wrapping up personal study, the application step almost always leads me to bow my heart in worship, confession, or thanksgiving. Or sometimes, I recognize a need in my life. Hence, the SIMPLY BIBLE daily format includes a place for *prayer*. Please use this! It may be the most important space of all.

Enjoy a lingering moment of being with God in His Word. Savor. Learn. Grow. Know. Thank. Praise. Confess. Yield. Love. Then carry a nugget of truth in your heart to ponder as you go about your day.

lesson *samples*

PRACTICE LESSONS & EXAMPLES

practice *lesson*

GENESIS 1:1-5

NOW IT'S YOUR TURN! Give it a try! Below are a few verses: Genesis 1:1-5. As you read, feel free to highlight, circle, underline, and mark up the text in whatever way you like. In the *Observe* column, jot down details that pop out and write down questions that come to mind. Then *Interpret*. Simply answer the questions you asked using the Scripture at hand or hop over to the toolkit: *Key Words*, *Definitions*, and *Cross References*. Use these as previously discussed to to help you better understand the meaning. Finish by summarizing, applying, and praying.

This is your workbook. The intent is to journal your thoughts as you engage with God and His Word. Don't be shy. Be you, be with God, and enjoy!

READ	OBSERVE	INTERPRET
[1] In the beginning, God created the heavens and the earth. [2] The earth was without form and void, and darkness was over the face of the deep. And the Spirit of God was hovering over the face of the waters. [3] And God said, "Let there be light," and there was light. [4] And God saw that the light was good. And God separated the light from the darkness. [5] God called the light Day, and the darkness he called Night. And there was evening and there was morning, the first day.		

KEY WORDS	DEFINITIONS	CROSS REFERENCES

MAIN POINT(S)	APPLY

PRAY

sample *lesson*

GENESIS 1:1-5 | FOR THOSE CRAZY, BUSY DAYS

We're busy. Life is hectic. Some days, you just don't have the time to go deep in your study. That's okay. One truth from God's Word transforms hearts, which often transforms the day. Using Genesis 1:1-5, here's what a study might look like with very little time. The goal is to observe, interpret, and apply just *one* thing (particularly about who God is):

READ	OBSERVE	INTERPRET
¹ In the beginning, God created the heavens and the earth. ² The earth was without form and void, and darkness was over the face of the deep. And the Spirit of God was hovering over the face of the waters. ³ And God said, "Let there be light," and there was light. ⁴ And God saw that the light was good. And God separated the light from the darkness. ⁵ God called the light Day, and the darkness he called Night. And there was evening and there was morning, the first day.	The Who? What do I learn about Him?	God! He's mentioned 6 times. - God was in the beginning. - God created. - His Spirit hovered. - He speaks. And there is light. - He sees: the light is good. - He separates: the light from the darkness - He calls (names) the light and darkness: day and night.

KEY WORDS	DEFINITIONS	CROSS REFERENCES
void	empty (NIV translation)	

MAIN POINT(S)

In the beginning, God created the heavens and earth.

APPLY

God, who was in the beginning, creates. Hovers. Speaks light. Separates light from darkness.

He still does that today. Praise Him! Thank Him!

PRAY

Creator God, I praise You! You were there in the beginning, hovering over the waters. I wonder what You thought as You hovered over the emptiness. Thank You for Your Creation. It's beautiful. Amazing. Lord, You spoke light into the darkness in the beginning. Would You please do that today? Help me to hear You and listen. Lead me in Your Light.

sample *lesson*

Do you have time to linger in God's Word? Using Genesis 1:1-5, here's an example of what a more extensive study could look like. Observe as much or as little as you like.

Remember: No two journals will look the same. There's so much more to observe!

READ	OBSERVE	INTERPRET
[1] In the beginning, God created the heavens and the earth. [2] The earth was without form and void, and darkness was over the face of the deep. And the Spirit of God was hovering over the face of the waters.	The Who?	God! He's mentioned 6 times.
	What do I learn about Him?	- God was in the beginning. - God created. - His Spirit hovered. - He speaks. And there is light. - He sees: the light is good. - He separates: the light from the darkness - He calls (names) the light and darkness: day and night.
	Earth- 2x Darkness- 3x Light- 5x	
[3] And God said, "Let there be light," and there was light. [4] And God saw that the light was good. And God separated the light from the darkness. [5] God called the light Day, and the darkness he called Night. And there was evening and there was morning, the first day.	When?	The beginning (when God created the heavens and the earth.)
	God says, "Let there be light" and then it exists! Who else can do this?! What power is this?	Light is significant. God saw it was good. Only God speaks and it is so. He is all powerful and almighty.

KEY WORDS	DEFINITIONS	CROSS REFERENCES
beginning	the point at which something begins, the start *(Webster's)*	John 1:1-3 In the beginning was the Word, and the Word was with God, and the Word was God. He was in the beginning with God. All things were made through him, and without him was not any thing made that was made.
created	to bring into existence *(Bible dictionary)*	
void	empty *(NIV translation)*	II Corinthians 4:6 For God, who said, "Let light shine out of darkness," has shone in our hearts to give the light of the knowledge of the glory of God in the face of Jesus Christ.
light	contrasted to darkness	
good	having desirable or positive qualities	

MAIN POINT(S)

In the beginning God created the heavens and the earth. He speaks light and there is light!

APPLY

Trust God. He was in the beginning. He creates beautiful things out of chaos and emptiness. He speaks light and it is so. He separates light from darkness. He still does that today. He can do this in my life and the lives of my loved ones. **Worship!** "Worthy are you, our Lord and God, to receive glory and honor and power, for you created all things, and by your will they existed and were created." *(Rev. 4:11)*

PRAY

Creator God, I praise You! You really are worthy of glory and honor and power, for in the beginning you created all things, and by your will they existed and were created. Thank You. Thank You for life and light. And thank You for Jesus, the True Light, Who was with You in the beginning. Your Spirit hovered over the emptiness, the waste, the chaos, and then, You spoke light into the darkness! That must have been AMAZING! Your ways are so far above mine. Please speak Your light into my life and the lives of these dear ones. Help us to hear You and listen. Lead us in Your Light

FOR WHERE YOU GO I WILL GO,
AND WHERE YOU LODGE I WILL LODGE.
YOUR PEOPLE SHALL BE MY PEOPLE,
AND YOUR GOD MY GOD.

RUTH 1:16

YOU DID IT! That's it. That's all there is to the SIMPLY BIBLE inductive process. If this is your first time, the process may feel a little awkward at first. Don't worry. You probably don't remember how clumsy and time-consuming it was the very first time you tried tying your shoe, riding a bike, or driving a car. Practice helps. The same will be true for Bible study. Like riding a bicycle, it gets easier.

Likewise, please know that your study guide will look different from most others. You are unique and special. And so, your observations and application will be unique. Every artist creates something different with a "blank page."

Indeed, you've probably gathered by now that this study is different. And different often falls outside our comfort zones. The purpose of this Bible study is that you may confidently read, understand, and apply God's Word like never before, using *simply the Bible*.

IT WILL REQUIRE A COMMITMENT. Would you please commit to finish this study book? By the end, with consistency, perseverance, and time spent with Him, you will better know God, His Word, and your identity in Him.

You're more observant, smarter, and stronger than you think you are. God created you that way. He desires to be known. He wants to show you that you are loved, valued, and never alone. Lean into Him. Ask, seek, and you will find. His grace is sufficient. His power is made perfect in our weakness.

> As the rain and the snow come down from heaven,
> and do not return to it without watering the earth
> and making it bud and flourish,
> so that it yields seed for the sower and bread for the eater,
>
> so is my word that goes out from my mouth:
> It will not return to me empty,
> but will accomplish what I desire
> and achieve the purpose for which I sent it.

> You will go out in joy and be led forth in peace;
> the mountains and hills will burst into song before you,
> and all the trees of the field will clap their hands.
>
> ISAIAH 55:10-12

Lord God Almighty, Thank You for Your Word! Like rain and snow watering the earth so that it might bud and flourish, may Your Word now water our hearts, minds, and souls, that our love for You and for one another would bud and flourish. May Your purposes and desires be accomplished. As we study with You, may we go out in joy and be led forth in Your peace. With all creation may we sing and clap for joy and bring glory to Your Name…

in *context*

EXAMINING THE CONTEXT OF **RUTH**

in *context*

EXAMINING THE CONTEXT OF **RUTH**

The story of Ruth takes place during the time of Judges, a time of apostasy when many Israelites had abandoned their faith in Yahweh in favor of foreign gods. In the midst of appalling unfaithfulness and chaos, the narrative of Ruth highlights faithfulness, loyalty, obedience, and generosity—qualities necessary to establish the royal line of King David, and, ultimately, King Jesus.

A key rule for studying Old Testament narrative is to remember that God is always the Hero. Although God's presence is subtle and remains largely unseen, Bible students will find this rule to be true in the story of Ruth. It is Yahweh Who rewards both faith and obedience. This God of the Israelites is shown to be merciful and gracious, steadfast in love and faithfulness, just as He originally revealed Himself to Moses:

> The LORD passed before [Moses] and proclaimed, "The LORD, the LORD, a God merciful and gracious, slow to anger, and abounding in steadfast love and faithfulness..."
>
> EXODUS 34:6

No specifics are found in the book to supply us with the precise time during Judges that this story takes place. Nonetheless, utilizing the genealogy at the end of Ruth, scholars place these events toward the end of the twelfth century BC, perhaps at the time of Jephthah.

Likewise, nothing mentions the book's author. Again, utilizing and recognizing that the genealogy listed at the end of the book does not include Solomon, some academics surmise that the book is authored during the reign of David. Fittingly, the book provides testimony of how David's heritage belonged to a family of faith, who chose obedient faithfulness to Yahweh, the God of the Israelites.

The story of Ruth opens in the country of Moab (Ruth 1). Very little is known about Ruth's kinsmen, the Moabites. As recorded in Genesis 19, these folks were related to Israel, having descended from Abraham's nephew, Lot. They occupied the land on the opposite side of the Dead Sea from the land of Judah. Although unfriendly towards the Israelites in the time of Moses (Numbers 21-25), they extended shelter to David when he was pursued by Saul (I Samuel 22). Later in Scripture, Moab was conquered by David (II Samuel 8:2). All the major prophets pronounced condemnation upon Moab (Jeremiah 48, Isaiah 15, Ezekiel 25), denouncing the worship of other gods.

An important cross-reference to understanding the context of the book of Ruth is found in Deuteronomy 25:5-10. This passage explains the laws given by God through Moses for Levirate marriage:

> 5 If brothers dwell together, and one of them dies and has no son, the wife of the dead man shall not be married outside the family to a stranger. Her husband's brother shall go in to her and take her as his wife and perform the duty of a husband's brother to her. 6 And the first son whom she bears shall succeed to the name of his dead brother, that his name may not be blotted out of Israel. 7 And if the man does not wish to take his brother's wife, then his brother's wife shall go up to the gate to the elders and say, 'My husband's brother refuses to perpetuate his brother's name in Israel; he will not perform the duty of a husband's brother to me.' 8 Then the elders of his city shall call him and speak to him, and if he persists, saying, 'I do not wish to take her,' 9 then his brother's wife shall go up to him in the presence of the elders and pull his sandal off his foot and spit in his face. And she shall answer and say, 'So shall it be done to the man who does not build up his brother's house.' 10 And the name of his house shall be called in Israel, 'The house of him who had his sandal pulled off.'

Simply defined, Levirate marriage involves a cross-cultural phenomenon whereby the nearest kinsman of a man who dies without sons marries his widow.[1] Although very strange to our 21st century sensibilities, God's plan provided protection for widows in the Ancient Near East culture. Without male protection, widows remained vulnerable and marginalized. This marriage provision demonstrates God's grace.

Throughout the laws and stories of the Old Testament, God's heart for orphans, widows, the poor, the vulnerable, the marginalized, and the suffering is revealed. This revelation culminates in the New Testament where God's heart to preserve and redeem broken people shines through Jesus Christ. God Himself becomes both a fellow sufferer and redeemer.

May God melt away any and all bitterness and bring comfort, peace, and joy as you study this book of Ruth.

---

[1] Pressler, C. (2000). *Levirate Marriage*. In D. N. Freedman, A. C. Myers, & A. B. Beck (Eds.), Eerdmans Dictionary of the Bible (p. 803). Grand Rapids, MI: W.B. Eerdmans.

a *challenge*

PURSUING NOBLE CHARACTER

a *challenge*

PURSUING NOBLE CHARACTER

Whenever we study Old Testament narrative, God stands as the Hero of the story. This is certainly true for the narrative of Ruth, that so beautifully exhibits God's provision, His steadfast love, and His mercy.

As we grow to better know and enjoy God through His Word, we also grow to better understand who we are as God's children and how we are called to live. Biblical narrative highlights spiritual lessons, to be gleaned from both God Himself and the characters of the story. We are always called to mirror the image of God. Concerning other characters, sometimes we find noble character to emulate. Other times, we clearly see what *not* to do.

The goal of this challenge is to help us more clearly understand and better apply the spiritual lessons found in Ruth. In the process, may our hearts be transformed and bear more noble character.

Each week, choose one character quality to define and better understand through a cross reference. Whether a positive or negative quality, identify how God and a character in the story of Ruth displays (or does not display) this quality. Identify this trait in yourself. Then practically apply what you learn to your life.

May God transform our hearts and our character to be more noble like His.

QUALITY: **BITTERNESS**

DEFINITION	CROSS REFERENCE

GOD	SOMEONE ELSE	YOU

LIFE APPLICATION

QUALITY: **LOYALTY**

DEFINITION	CROSS REFERENCE

GOD	SOMEONE ELSE	YOU

LIFE APPLICATION

QUALITY: **OBEDIENCE**	
DEFINITION	CROSS REFERENCE

GOD	SOMEONE ELSE	YOU

LIFE APPLICATION

QUALITY: **GENEROSITY**	
DEFINITION	CROSS REFERENCE

GOD	SOMEONE ELSE	YOU

LIFE APPLICATION

I WILL DO FOR YOU
ALL THAT YOU ASK....

RUTH 3:11

draw a *map*

USE THIS PAGE TO DRAW YOUR OWN MAP OF ISRAEL

chapter *one*

RUTH 1

take *note*

RUTH 1

take *note*

RUTH 1

day *one*

RUTH 1:1-5

READ	OBSERVE	INTERPRET
[1] In the days when the judges ruled there was a famine in the land, and a man of Bethlehem in Judah went to sojourn in the country of Moab, he and his wife and his two sons. [2] The name of the man was Elimelech and the name of his wife Naomi, and the names of his two sons were Mahlon and Chilion. They were Ephrathites from Bethlehem in Judah. They went into the country of Moab and remained there. [3] But Elimelech, the husband of Naomi, died, and she was left with her two sons. [4] These took Moabite wives; the name of the one was Orpah and the name of the other Ruth. They lived there about ten years, [5] and both Mahlon and Chilion died, so that the woman was left without her two sons and her husband.		

KEY WORDS	DEFINITIONS	CROSS REFERENCES

MAIN POINT(S)	APPLY

PRAY

day *two*

RUTH 1:6-14

READ

⁶ Then she arose with her daughters-in-law to return from the country of Moab, for she had heard in the fields of Moab that the Lord had visited his people and given them food. ⁷ So she set out from the place where she was with her two daughters-in-law, and they went on the way to return to the land of Judah. ⁸ But Naomi said to her two daughters-in-law, "Go, return each of you to her mother's house. May the Lord deal kindly with you, as you have dealt with the dead and with me. ⁹ The Lord grant that you may find rest, each of you in the house of her husband!" Then she kissed them, and they lifted up their voices and wept. ¹⁰ And they said to her, "No, we will return with you to your people." ¹¹ But Naomi said, "Turn back, my daughters; why will you go with me? Have I yet sons in my womb that they may become your husbands? ¹² Turn back, my daughters; go your way, for I am too old to have a husband. If I should say I have hope, even if I should have a husband this night and should bear sons, ¹³ would you therefore wait till they were grown? Would you therefore refrain from marrying? No, my daughters, for it is exceedingly bitter to me for your sake that the hand of the Lord has gone out against me." ¹⁴ Then they lifted up their voices and wept again. And Orpah kissed her mother-in-law, but Ruth clung to her.

OBSERVE

INTERPRET

KEY WORDS	DEFINITIONS	CROSS REFERENCES

MAIN POINT(S)

APPLY

PRAY

day *three*

READ	OBSERVE	INTERPRET
[15] And she said, "See, your sister-in-law has gone back to her people and to her gods; return after your sister-in-law." [16] But Ruth said, "Do not urge me to leave you or to return from following you. For where you go I will go, and where you lodge I will lodge. Your people shall be my people, and your God my God. [17] Where you die I will die, and there will I be buried. May the Lord do so to me and more also if anything but death parts me from you." [18] And when Naomi saw that she was determined to go with her, she said no more.		

KEY WORDS	DEFINITIONS	CROSS REFERENCES

MAIN POINT(S)

APPLY

PRAY

day *four*

READ	OBSERVE	INTERPRET
19 So the two of them went on until they came to Bethlehem. And when they came to Bethlehem, the whole town was stirred because of them. And the women said, "Is this Naomi?" 20 She said to them, "Do not call me Naomi; call me Mara for the Almighty has dealt very bitterly with me. 21 I went away full, and the Lord has brought me back empty. Why call me Naomi, when the Lord has testified against me and the Almighty has brought calamity upon me?" 22 So Naomi returned, and Ruth the Moabite her daughter-in-law with her, who returned from the country of Moab. And they came to Bethlehem at the beginning of barley harvest.		

KEY WORDS	DEFINITIONS	CROSS REFERENCES

MAIN POINT(S)

APPLY

PRAY

day *five*

RUTH 1 | REVIEW & DISCUSSION QUESTIONS

1 Summary:	2 Write out your favorite verse from the passage, perhaps in your own words:
3 Name the characters introduced in this story and where they are from.	4 Who dies at the beginning of this story? Where are the widows located?
5 Draw a simple map of Israel on page 46. Mark both the country of Moab and the town of Bethlehem. Draw a dotted line denoting a possible route from Moab to Bethlehem.	6 Why does Naomi decide to go to the land of Judah? What is the reaction of her daughters-in-law?

7 Why is it a big deal for Orpah and Ruth to leave Moab?

8 Why do you think Ruth clings to her mother-in-law and refuses to leave her? Explain using Scripture.

9 Try to put yourself in the shoes of Naomi and Ruth in the context of the Ancient Near East. Describe the journey for these two women.

10 How do the people of Bethlehem react to Naomi and Ruth's return? Why?

11 Why does Naomi change her name? Is her view of God true? Explain.

12 What do you learn about God from this chapter? In the midst of the tragedy of this story, can you find reason to praise God?

take it to *heart*

USE THIS SPACE TO WRITE OUT A FAVORITE VERSE OR PASSAGE FROM THIS WEEK'S STUDY, OR SIMPLY JOURNAL AND SHARE YOUR HEART WITH GOD ABOUT WHAT YOU ARE LEARNING.

MAY HE BE BLESSED BY
THE LORD, WHOSE KINDNESS
HAS NOT FORSAKEN THE
LIVING OR THE DEAD!

RUTH 2:20

chapter *two*

RUTH 2

take *note*

take *note*

NOTES ON RUTH 2

day *one*

RUTH 2:1-7

READ

¹ Now Naomi had a relative of her husband's, a worthy man of the clan of Elimelech, whose name was Boaz. ² And Ruth the Moabite said to Naomi, "Let me go to the field and glean among the ears of grain after him in whose sight I shall find favor." And she said to her, "Go, my daughter." ³ So she set out and went and gleaned in the field after the reapers, and she happened to come to the part of the field belonging to Boaz, who was of the clan of Elimelech. ⁴ And behold, Boaz came from Bethlehem. And he said to the reapers, "The Lord be with you!" And they answered, "The Lord bless you." ⁵ Then Boaz said to his young man who was in charge of the reapers, "Whose young woman is this?" ⁶ And the servant who was in charge of the reapers answered, "She is the young Moabite woman, who came back with Naomi from the country of Moab. ⁷ She said, 'Please let me glean and gather among the sheaves after the reapers.' So she came, and she has continued from early morning until now, except for a short rest."

OBSERVE

INTERPRET

KEY WORDS	DEFINITIONS	CROSS REFERENCES

MAIN POINT(S)

APPLY

PRAY

day *two*

READ

8 Then Boaz said to Ruth, "Now, listen, my daughter, do not go to glean in another field or leave this one, but keep close to my young women. 9 Let your eyes be on the field that they are reaping, and go after them. Have I not charged the young men not to touch you? And when you are thirsty, go to the vessels and drink what the young men have drawn." 10 Then she fell on her face, bowing to the ground, and said to him, "Why have I found favor in your eyes, that you should take notice of me, since I am a foreigner?" 11 But Boaz answered her, "All that you have done for your mother-in-law since the death of your husband has been fully told to me, and how you left your father and mother and your native land and came to a people that you did not know before. 12 The Lord repay you for what you have done, and a full reward be given you by the Lord, the God of Israel, under whose wings you have come to take refuge!" 13 Then she said, "I have found favor in your eyes, my lord, for you have comforted me and spoken kindly to your servant, though I am not one of your servants."

OBSERVE

INTERPRET

KEY WORDS	DEFINITIONS	CROSS REFERENCES

MAIN POINT(S)

APPLY

PRAY

day *three*

RUTH 2:14-16

READ	OBSERVE	INTERPRET
¹⁴ And at mealtime Boaz said to her, "Come here and eat some bread and dip your morsel in the wine." So she sat beside the reapers, and he passed to her roasted grain. And she ate until she was satisfied, and she had some left over. ¹⁵ When she rose to glean, Boaz instructed his young men, saying, "Let her glean even among the sheaves, and do not reproach her. ¹⁶ And also pull out some from the bundles for her and leave it for her to glean, and do not rebuke her."		

KEY WORDS	DEFINITIONS	CROSS REFERENCES

MAIN POINT(S)

APPLY

PRAY

day *four*

READ

¹⁷ So she gleaned in the field until evening. Then she beat out what she had gleaned, and it was about an ephah of barley. ¹⁸ And she took it up and went into the city. Her mother-in-law saw what she had gleaned. She also brought out and gave her what food she had left over after being satisfied. ¹⁹ And her mother-in-law said to her, "Where did you glean today? And where have you worked? Blessed be the man who took notice of you." So she told her mother-in-law with whom she had worked and said, "The man's name with whom I worked today is Boaz." ²⁰ And Naomi said to her daughter-in-law, "May he be blessed by the Lord, whose kindness has not forsaken the living or the dead!" Naomi also said to her, "The man is a close relative of ours, one of our redeemers." ²¹ And Ruth the Moabite said, "Besides, he said to me, 'You shall keep close by my young men until they have finished all my harvest.'" ²² And Naomi said to Ruth, her daughter-in-law, "It is good, my daughter, that you go out with his young women, lest in another field you be assaulted." ²³ So she kept close to the young women of Boaz, gleaning until the end of the barley and wheat harvests. And she lived with her mother-in-law.

OBSERVE

INTERPRET

KEY WORDS	DEFINITIONS	CROSS REFERENCES

MAIN POINT(S)	APPLY

PRAY

day *five*

RUTH 2 | REVIEW & DISCUSSION QUESTIONS

1 Summary:	2 Write out your favorite verse from the passage, perhaps in your own words:
3 Name the new character introduced in Ruth 2:1. How is he described?	4 What does Ruth offer to do?
5 In this context, explain the difference between gleaning and reaping. (2:2-3)	6 Deuteronomy 24:19 provides a cross reference for Ruth 2:2. What does God's law reveal about His heart?

7 What instructions does Boaz give Ruth? What specifically is Boaz providing for Ruth? What is Ruth's reaction?

8 How does Boaz explain his generosity in Ruth 2:11-12?

9 Who does Boaz point to as Ruth's refuge? What do you learn about Boaz's view of God?

10 How else does Boaz display kindness to Ruth? (2:14-16) Why are his actions significant?

11 Explain Naomi's meaning when she refers to Boaz as "one of our redeemers." (2:20)

12 What do you learn about God from this chapter? In the midst of the tragedy of this story, can you find reason to praise God?

take it to *heart*

USE THIS SPACE TO WRITE OUT A FAVORITE VERSE OR PASSAGE FROM THIS WEEK'S STUDY, OR SIMPLY JOURNAL AND SHARE YOUR HEART WITH GOD ABOUT WHAT YOU ARE LEARNING.

I WILL DO FOR YOU ALL THAT
YOU ASK, FOR ALL MY FELLOW
TOWNSMEN KNOW THAT YOU
ARE A WORTHY WOMAN.

RUTH 3:11

chapter *three*

RUTH 3

take *note*

take *note*

NOTES ON RUTH 3

day *one*

READ	OBSERVE	INTERPRET
¹ Then Naomi her mother-in-law said to her, "My daughter, should I not seek rest for you, that it may be well with you? ² Is not Boaz our relative, with whose young women you were? See, he is winnowing barley tonight at the threshing floor. ³ Wash therefore and anoint yourself, and put on your cloak and go down to the threshing floor, but do not make yourself known to the man until he has finished eating and drinking. ⁴ But when he lies down, observe the place where he lies. Then go and uncover his feet and lie down, and he will tell you what to do." ⁵ And she replied, "All that you say I will do."		

KEY WORDS	DEFINITIONS	CROSS REFERENCES

MAIN POINT(S)

APPLY

PRAY

day *two*

RUTH 3:6-9

READ	OBSERVE	INTERPRET
⁶ So she went down to the threshing floor and did just as her mother-in-law had commanded her. ⁷ And when Boaz had eaten and drunk, and his heart was merry, he went to lie down at the end of the heap of grain. Then she came softly and uncovered his feet and lay down. ⁸ At midnight the man was startled and turned over, and behold, a woman lay at his feet! ⁹ He said, "Who are you?" And she answered, "I am Ruth, your servant. Spread your wings over your servant, for you are a redeemer."		

KEY WORDS	DEFINITIONS	CROSS REFERENCES

MAIN POINT(S)

APPLY

PRAY

day *three*

RUTH 3:10-13

READ	OBSERVE	INTERPRET
10 And he said, "May you be blessed by the Lord, my daughter. You have made this last kindness greater than the first in that you have not gone after young men, whether poor or rich. 11 And now, my daughter, do not fear. I will do for you all that you ask, for all my fellow townsmen know that you are a worthy woman. 12 And now it is true that I am a redeemer. Yet there is a redeemer nearer than I. 13 Remain tonight, and in the morning, if he will redeem you, good; let him do it. But if he is not willing to redeem you, then, as the Lord lives, I will redeem you. Lie down until the morning."		

KEY WORDS	DEFINITIONS	CROSS REFERENCES

MAIN POINT(S)

APPLY

PRAY

day *four*

RUTH 3:14-18

READ	OBSERVE	INTERPRET
[14] So she lay at his feet until the morning, but arose before one could recognize another. And he said, "Let it not be known that the woman came to the threshing floor." [15] And he said, "Bring the garment you are wearing and hold it out." So she held it, and he measured out six measures of barley and put it on her. Then she went into the city. [16] And when she came to her mother-in-law, she said, "How did you fare, my daughter?" Then she told her all that the man had done for her, [17] saying, "These six measures of barley he gave to me, for he said to me, 'You must not go back empty-handed to your mother-in-law.'" [18] She replied, "Wait, my daughter, until you learn how the matter turns out, for the man will not rest but will settle the matter today."		

KEY WORDS	DEFINITIONS	CROSS REFERENCES

MAIN POINT(S)	APPLY

PRAY

day *five*

RUTH 3 | REVIEW & DISCUSSION QUESTIONS

1 Summary:	2 Write out your favorite verse from the passage, perhaps in your own words:
3 What "rest" is Naomi referring to in Ruth 3:1? Explain how this rest is cultural in the Ancient Near East.	4 Sometimes cultural ideas are passed on. Often, people seek "rest" through marriage, but where does true biblical "rest" lie today? Explain using Scripture if possible.
5 In verse 5, Ruth tells Naomi, "All that you say I will do." What do you learn about Ruth's character?	6 Both Naomi and Boaz have referred to Ruth as "daughter," a term of endearment. She is a foreigner in a foreign land. What feelings or assurance might this evoke in Ruth? Apply.

7 Ruth does everything as Naomi suggests. What is Ruth's bold request in verse 9? What else do you learn of Ruth's character?

8 How does Boaz respond?

9 What is the "first kindness" that Boaz refers to in Ruth 3:10? *(For a cross reference, consider Ruth 1:8.)* Why is this kindness even greater?

10 Define *worthy*. (3:11) Describe the qualities that make Ruth worthy. Apply.

11 Explain Naomi's reply in Ruth 3:18.

12 What do you learn about God from this chapter? In the midst of the tragedy of this story, can you find reason to praise God?

take it to *heart*

USE THIS SPACE TO WRITE OUT A FAVORITE VERSE OR PASSAGE
FROM THIS WEEK'S STUDY, OR SIMPLY JOURNAL AND SHARE
YOUR HEART WITH GOD ABOUT WHAT YOU ARE LEARNING.

SO BOAZ TOOK RUTH,
AND SHE BECAME HIS WIFE.

RUTH 4:13

chapter *four*

RUTH 4

take *note*

NOTES ON RUTH 4

take *note*

NOTES ON RUTH 4

day *one*

RUTH 4:1-6

READ

¹ Now Boaz had gone up to the gate and sat down there. And behold, the redeemer, of whom Boaz had spoken, came by. So Boaz said, "Turn aside, friend; sit down here." And he turned aside and sat down. ² And he took ten men of the elders of the city and said, "Sit down here." So they sat down. ³ Then he said to the redeemer, "Naomi, who has come back from the country of Moab, is selling the parcel of land that belonged to our relative Elimelech. ⁴ So I thought I would tell you of it and say, 'Buy it in the presence of those sitting here and in the presence of the elders of my people.' If you will redeem it, redeem it. But if you will not, tell me, that I may know, for there is no one besides you to redeem it, and I come after you." And he said, "I will redeem it." ⁵ Then Boaz said, "The day you buy the field from the hand of Naomi, you also acquire Ruth the Moabite, the widow of the dead, in order to perpetuate the name of the dead in his inheritance." ⁶ Then the redeemer said, "I cannot redeem it for myself, lest I impair my own inheritance. Take my right of redemption yourself, for I cannot redeem it."

OBSERVE

INTERPRET

KEY WORDS	DEFINITIONS	CROSS REFERENCES

MAIN POINT(S)	APPLY

PRAY

day *two*

READ	OBSERVE	INTERPRET
7 Now this was the custom in former times in Israel concerning redeeming and exchanging: to confirm a transaction, the one drew off his sandal and gave it to the other, and this was the manner of attesting in Israel. 8 So when the redeemer said to Boaz, "Buy it for yourself," he drew off his sandal. 9 Then Boaz said to the elders and all the people, "You are witnesses this day that I have bought from the hand of Naomi all that belonged to Elimelech and all that belonged to Chilion and to Mahlon. 10 Also Ruth the Moabite, the widow of Mahlon, I have bought to be my wife, to perpetuate the name of the dead in his inheritance, that the name of the dead may not be cut off from among his brothers and from the gate of his native place. You are witnesses this day."		

KEY WORDS	DEFINITIONS	CROSS REFERENCES

MAIN POINT(S)

APPLY

PRAY

day *three*

READ

¹¹ Then all the people who were at the gate and the elders said, "We are witnesses. May the Lord make the woman, who is coming into your house, like Rachel and Leah, who together built up the house of Israel. May you act worthily in Ephrathah and be renowned in Bethlehem, ¹² and may your house be like the house of Perez, whom Tamar bore to Judah, because of the offspring that the Lord will give you by this young woman."

¹³ So Boaz took Ruth, and she became his wife. And he went in to her, and the Lord gave her conception, and she bore a son. ¹⁴ Then the women said to Naomi, "Blessed be the Lord, who has not left you this day without a redeemer, and may his name be renowned in Israel! ¹⁵ He shall be to you a restorer of life and a nourisher of your old age, for your daughter-in-law who loves you, who is more to you than seven sons, has given birth to him." ¹⁶ Then Naomi took the child and laid him on her lap and became his nurse. ¹⁷ And the women of the neighborhood gave him a name, saying, "A son has been born to Naomi." They named him Obed. He was the father of Jesse, the father of David.

OBSERVE

INTERPRET

KEY WORDS	DEFINITIONS	CROSS REFERENCES

MAIN POINT(S)

APPLY

PRAY

day *four*

READ	OBSERVE	INTERPRET
[18] Now these are the generations of Perez: Perez fathered Hezron, [19] Hezron fathered Ram, Ram fathered Amminadab, [20] Amminadab fathered Nahshon, Nahshon fathered Salmon, [21] Salmon fathered Boaz, Boaz fathered Obed, [22] Obed fathered Jesse, and Jesse fathered David.		

KEY WORDS	DEFINITIONS	CROSS REFERENCES

MAIN POINT(S)	APPLY

PRAY

day *five*

1 Summary:	2 Write out your favorite verse from the passage, perhaps in your own words:
3 This chapter begins with Boaz going to the city gate. Who does he gather together and why?	4 Ruth and Naomi's closer redeemer opts to redeem the land that Naomi is selling, but then backs away. Why?
5 In what interesting way is the legal transaction certified?	6 What three things does Boaz redeem and what does he vow to do before the witnesses?

7 How do the witnesses respond? What blessing do they bestow upon Ruth?

8 How does the Lord bless Boaz and Ruth? Who else is blessed?

9 Who do the women glorify? What do they proclaim to Naomi about God and what He has done?

10 Who names the baby and what do they name him? How do the women describe Ruth?

11 Why is Obed's genealogy listed? Does this genealogy say anything else about God?

12 What do you learn about God from this chapter? In the midst of the tragedy of this story, can you find reason to praise God?

take it to *heart*

USE THIS SPACE TO WRITE OUT A FAVORITE VERSE OR PASSAGE
FROM THIS WEEK'S STUDY, OR SIMPLY JOURNAL AND SHARE
YOUR HEART WITH GOD ABOUT WHAT YOU ARE LEARNING.

MAY THE LORD MAKE THE WOMAN,
WHO IS COMING INTO YOUR HOUSE,
LIKE RACHEL AND LEAH, WHO TOGETHER
BUILT UP THE HOUSE OF ISRAEL.

RUTH 4:11

final *thoughts*

WRAPPING UP

final *thoughts*

1 Choose your favorite verse from the book of Ruth. Write it out here.	2 Why is this verse meaningful to you?
3 Provide a final, but brief character analysis of each of the main characters: Ruth, Naomi, and Boaz.	4 Which character would you most like to emulate and why?
5 What overarching theme or themes did you notice throughout your study?	6 A notable theme in the book of Ruth is the kinsman redeemer. Explain what you learned.

7 Relate how Boaz foreshadows Jesus Christ as our Kinsman Redeemer.

8 Despite God not being seen much in the book of Ruth, what did you learn about Him?

9 How would you summarize the book of Ruth in one sentence? Could you summarize this book in one word?

10 How does Ruth fit into the "Big View" of the Bible?

11 How has God transformed your heart through this study of Ruth? How will you live or think differently than before?

12 Praise God for at least one truth He has revealed in the course of this study:

BLESSED BE THE LORD,
WHO HAS NOT LEFT YOU THIS DAY
WITHOUT A REDEEMER...

RUTH 4:14

leader *guide*

MAXIMIZING THE SMALL-GROUP EXPERIENCE

GO THEREFORE AND MAKE
DISCIPLES OF ALL NATIONS,
BAPTIZING THEM IN THE
NAME OF THE FATHER AND
OF THE SON AND OF THE
HOLY SPIRIT, TEACHING THEM
TO OBSERVE ALL THAT I
HAVE COMMANDED YOU.

MATTHEW 28:19-20

introduction

LEADING WOMEN THROUGH **SIMPLY BIBLE**

Welcome to SIMPLY BIBLE! Thank you for your commitment to walk alongside others for this season of exploring God's Word. In my own life, God has proven Himself faithful. Time and again, as I step out in faith to lead and seek to be a blessing to others, the blessing seems to always be mine. He is gracious that way. So, it is my heartfelt prayer for leaders that as you seek to be a blessing, you, too, will be blessed beyond measure by the experience of shepherding others through God's Word. Truly, what a privilege to facilitate conversations that point to Christ!

The primary objective of SIMPLY BIBLE is this:

> To inspire every woman to love God with all her heart, soul, mind and strength, and to love others as herself.
>
> LUKE 10:27

And you, the small-group leader, will play an important role in inspiring Bible students to do exactly that! You will lead your group through meaningful conversations, with the help of the discussion questions found at the end of every chapter in this workbook. The intent is to help others grow and connect with Jesus and with one another, gently guiding them to authentic relationships and unity.

Our goal for study is to see others growing in relationship with Christ and one another. You do not need to be a Bible expert to lead discussions about His Word; you only need a heart to love and encourage. So what does effective small-group leadership look like?

GUARDING YOUR HEART. *Ethos* is a Latin word that denotes the fundamental character or spirit of a community, group or person. When used to discuss dramatic literature, ethos is that moral element used to determine a character's action rather than his or her thought or emotion. [1] Ethos points to the inward being, to the moral fabric of the heart. In Biblical language, ethos absolutely compares to a person's heart. And our hearts are important to God.

His Word tells us:

> Above all else, guard your heart,
> for everything you do flows from it.
>
> PROVERBS 4:23 (NIV)

Above all else, guard your heart. Why? Because everything we do flows from the heart, from our inward being. And that "everything" includes leading others through God's Word. If we want to see men and women growing in authentic relationships with Christ and with one another, that process must first begin in our own hearts.

> For the Lord sees not as man sees: man looks on the
> outward appearance, but the Lord looks on the heart.
>
> 1 SAMUEL 16:7

So often, as individuals and as ministry groups, we get caught up in appearances. I'm guilty. How easy is it, as leaders, to dress ourselves for Bible study, look nice on the outside, make the tables or Zoom background look inviting, share pleasant words, fill in the blank spaces of our studies, and all the while never touch the core of our hearts? God looks at the heart. Perhaps we should, too.

---

[1] **ethos.** Dictionary.com. *Dictionary.com Unabridged.* Random House, Inc. http://www.dictionary.com/browse/ethos (accessed: March 16, 2018).

Truly, there is much to share concerning effectively "guarding our hearts" while leading others in inductive Bible study. However, for our purposes today, let's keep things simple and limit our necessary ingredients to three:

(1) Jesus
(2) Prayer
(3) The Word

By guarding our hearts in these ways, successful Bible study leadership is certain. Let's briefly seek to understand.

GUARDING YOUR HEART WITH JESUS

This may seem obvious, even "in your face" obvious. But honestly, isn't it easy for us to miss the forest for the trees? How can we expect our flocks to believe if we ourselves are not believing? Without Jesus and His Word dwelling in our hearts, we will not overflow with Him and His Spirit. Our efforts will ring hollow. Paul puts it this way:

> If I speak in the tongues of men and of angels, but have not love, I am a noisy gong or a clanging cymbal.
>
> 1 CORINTHIANS 13:1

None of us wants to annoy others as a gong gone wrong. But without a personal heart connection to God's heart of love, we labor in our own strength. A friend referred to this kind of fruit as being like the "fake grapes" found in her Grandma's kitchen. Rather, we are after the juicy-sweet fruit of the Spirit that comes from abiding in the True Vine.

> Abide in me, and I in you. As the branch cannot bear fruit by itself, unless it abides in the vine, neither can you, unless you abide in me.
>
> JOHN 15:4

To overflow with Christ, one must first abide in Him. Abiding in Jesus is the secret, powerful ingredient to leading Bible study. Okay, maybe it's not so secret, but it is powerful! Some days we feel that heart connection with God and other days we do not, but we can know we are abiding when we are obeying and seeking to follow His will. Fruit will follow.

Are you daily abiding with The Word from the inside out? Our character and our inner lives ought to align with our outward appearance. There is nothing more effective than a leader leading others with a humble and authentic heart. This transformation happens as we apply Scripture, yield to God's will and allow for the Spirit's holy work to happen within our own hearts. That leads to true beauty. It's super attractive. Others will want to follow. Peter says it this way:

> Let your adorning be the hidden person of the heart
> with the imperishable beauty of a gentle and quiet spirit,
> which in God's sight is very precious.
>
> I PETER 3:4

GUARDING YOUR HEART WITH **PRAYER**

Here again, the need for prayer is obvious, but sometimes when we get caught up in the preparation details, we overlook the obvious. Pray, pray, and pray! If Jesus required prayer in order to remain in relationship and united with the Father in His mission, we surely require it more. Prayer helps us to stay focused on Christ and remember that He is the One who leads the way. However, without Christ to do the heavy lifting of paving the way and clearing the path, we will struggle to get there. And so, we pray.

Set aside time to pray for Bible study. Even before the semester begins, take one day away from other activities to commune with God committing the weeks of study to Him. Remember that prayer is simply sharing your heart and relating with God. It involves both speaking and listening. If leading a group in prayer, I find using the acronym P.R.A.Y. to be useful. This template allows groups to walk through four steps of prayer:

P	PRAISE	Praise God for who He is.

Blessed are those who have learned to acclaim you...
Psalm 89:15 NIV

In a group, it is effective to use short "popcorn prayers" of praise where everyone takes turns utilizing simple words and phrases to worship God as the Spirit leads.

- I praise You, God, as the Light of the World.
- I praise You for You are Mighty to Save.
- Lord, You are Life.
- You are Truth.

Beginning group sessions with praise turns our hearts toward God.

R	REPENT	Confess and agree with God concerning sin.

If we confess our sins, he is faithful and just to forgive
us our sins and to cleanse us from all unrighteousness.
I John 1:9

Offer group members a silent moment to allow for private confession.

A	ADORE	Admire and thank God for His ways.

Let us come into his presence with thanksgiving;
let us make a joyful noise to him with songs of praise!
Psalm 95:2

Thanksgiving is a beautiful way to end a Bible study session Together, give thanks for all that God has revealed during your study.

Y	YIELD	Acknowledge your dependence on God. Yield to His ways.

Whoever abides in me and I in him, he it is that bears
much fruit, for apart from me you can do nothing.
John 15:5

Abide in the Lord and give every concern to Him!

With that, what sorts of things shall we yield to God? Here are a few ideas and ways to align with God's heart:

- May God be glorified through the study.
- May God's will be accomplished in our hearts.
- May we know, believe, and abide in Christ and His love.
- May our hearts be united with His and with one another.
- May God protect us from all distractions as we study His Word.
- May God's Word transform hearts and lives.
- May He offer His help as we seek to obey and be holy, as He is holy.

GUARDING YOUR HEART WITH **THE WORD**

Read. Reflect. Remember His Word. Whether teaching a large group or facilitating discussion in a small group, it's easy for leaders to fall into the trap of thinking that we need to have all the right answers. Furthermore, we often feel the need to be able to speak all those answers eloquently. Due to this false thinking, many leaders spend countless hours scouring commentaries. And we wear ourselves out! After all, God's Word is so deep and rich that we will not plumb the depths of a Scripture passage in just one week. Thinking we need to have all the right answers is a fallacy.

Without a doubt, commentaries have their valuable place for solid interpretation. (Interpretation is that portion of inductive study where everyone should all be on the same page.) However, the risk for leaders who spend too much time delving into commentaries is that their workbook journals, teaching, and discussion times tend to reflect the commentaries versus Scripture itself. Rather, it is always more effective to share how God has transformed your heart directly through His Word.

As we read, observe and marinate in the Bible text itself, God's Spirit teaches and leads. His Word speaks on its own. It's powerful and effective. We can trust in it!

> So shall my word be that goes out from my mouth;
> it shall not return to me empty, but it shall
> accomplish that which I purpose, and shall
> succeed in the thing for which I sent it.
>
> ISAIAH 55:11

Read, read, and read again. As mentioned in the introduction, read the Scripture passage using various translations. Read aloud, and read slowly. Ponder. Listen to the Word while driving. Talk about what you are learning and discovering about God with family and friends. This will help you be prepared to share your heart when time for Bible study. Just as we marinate meat to soften, tenderize and flavor it, we "sit in" the text allowing God's Spirit to soften, tenderize and flavor our hearts and minds with His personal message.

> I have stored up your word in my heart,
> that I might not sin against you.
>
> PSALM 119:11

A challenging but brilliant way to soak in Scripture is memorization. It's hard work, but the payoff is great. Scripture becomes embedded within us and can overflow from the heart when needed. Memorized scriptures guard my own heart. In leading, I've noticed that reciting Scripture over women deeply touches their hearts in a way that nothing else does. I highly recommend memorizing at least one key verse from any study.

Ideally, when studying in groups, teachers and small group leaders should prepare the study a week ahead of time. Yep! You read that right. Seek to be one week ahead of the regular study schedule. Then allow time for leaders to review together before leading and teaching in groups the following week. The benefits of discussing, sharing, and grappling with the Word as leaders are priceless for preparation and confidence in leading. Also, through that time, God will knit together the hearts of the leaders. That dynamic will then transform the *ethos* or heart of the group as a whole.

GUARDING HEARTS WITH JESUS, PRAYER, AND HIS WORD prepares us for life changing and dynamic conversations around our Bible study tables or Zoom groups. In fact, by communing with Jesus and His Spirit through prayer and His Word, you truly have all you need in order to successfully lead a group.

> But you will receive power when the Holy Spirit
> has come upon you, and you will be my witnesses
> in Jerusalem and in all Judea and Samaria,
> and to the end of the earth.
>
> ACTS 1:8

The following tools and resources included in this appendix may provide additional help and support as you endeavor to lead your group. Use them however you find them to be helpful.

- Effective Leadership Guide
- Weekly Preparation Guide
- Bible Study Schedule
- Small Group Roster
- Attendance Record
- Prayer Log

effective *leadership*

A GUIDE TO LEADING A SMALL GROUP EFFECTIVELY

Remember that the goal for our study is to see women growing in relationship with Christ and one another. You do not need to be a Bible expert to lead women in discussion about His Word. You only need a heart to love and encourage women. So, what does effective small group leadership look like?

ENCOURAGING | In an encouraging small group, all participants feel included and welcome to share freely. Thoughts and ideas are respected, and women are cheered on in their efforts to grow closer to God through their study of His Word.

BIBLICALLY SOUND | When we endeavor to create a biblically-sound environment, we point women in the direction of truth and correct doctrine, gently guiding them away from wrong thinking.

BALANCED | In a group that is balanced, shy or quiet women are drawn out and encouraged to participate in discussions, while "over-sharers" are encouraged to listen to others and not to dominate the conversation.

WISE | A wise small group leader recognizes when the conversation is getting off-topic or veering toward gossip. In such situations, it is a good idea to redirect women back to the ultimate focus of the meeting: God's Word.

PRAYERFUL | A prayerful group leader is an asset to her group. She prays regularly for her group members and facilitates opportunities for them to pray for one another.

CONFIDENTIAL | Group members should feel secure that the things they share will remain confidential. An effective small group leader is committed to preserving the privacy of her group members.

weekly preparation guide
PREPARING FOR SMALL-GROUP MEETINGS

WEEK 1: RUTH 1

☐ Read the assigned daily passages.

☐ Use each daily framework to observe, interpret, and apply.

☐ Respond to all of the Day 5 questions.

☐ Pray for your small group meeting and for your group members.

1 What does this week's study tell me about God?	2 What does this week's study tell me about how I am to relate to Him?

WEEK 2: RUTH 2

☐ Read the assigned daily passages.

☐ Use each daily framework to observe, interpret, and apply.

☐ Respond to all of the Day 5 questions.

☐ Pray for your small group meeting and for your group members.

1 What does this week's study tell me about God?	2 What does this week's study tell me about how I am to relate to Him?

WEEK 3: RUTH 3

☐   Read the assigned daily passages.

☐   Use each daily framework to observe, interpret, and apply.

☐   Respond to all of the Day 5 questions.

☐   Pray for your small group meeting and for your group members.

1 What does this week's study tell me about God?	2 What does this week's study tell me about how I am to relate to Him?

WEEK 4: RUTH 4

☐   Read the assigned daily passages.

☐   Use each daily framework to observe, interpret, and apply.

☐   Respond to all of the Day 5 questions.

☐   Pray for your small group meeting and for your group members.

1 What does this week's study tell me about God?	2 What does this week's study tell me about how I am to relate to Him?

WEEK 5: FINAL THOUGHTS

☐ Read the assigned daily passages.

☐ Use each daily framework to observe, interpret, and apply.

☐ Respond to all of the Day 5 questions.

☐ Pray for your small group meeting and for your group members.

1 What does this week's study tell me about God?	2 What does this week's study tell me about how I am to relate to Him?

bible study *schedule*

RUTH | A **SIMPLY BIBLE** STUDY

	READING ASSIGNMENT	SMALL GROUP MEETING DATE	LEADER MEETING DATE
WEEK 1			
WEEK 2			
WEEK 3			
WEEK 4			
WEEK 5			

small group *roster*

RUTH | A **SIMPLY BIBLE** STUDY

PARTICIPANT LIST

1

2

3

4

5

6

7

8

9

10

11

12

13

14

15

NAME

BIRTHDAY	
PHONE NUMBER	
EMAIL ADDRESS	
CONTACT METHOD	

NOTES

NAME

BIRTHDAY	
PHONE NUMBER	
EMAIL ADDRESS	
CONTACT METHOD	

NOTES

NAME

BIRTHDAY	
PHONE NUMBER	
EMAIL ADDRESS	
CONTACT METHOD	

NOTES

NAME

BIRTHDAY

PHONE NUMBER

EMAIL ADDRESS

CONTACT METHOD

NOTES

NAME

BIRTHDAY

PHONE NUMBER

EMAIL ADDRESS

CONTACT METHOD

NOTES

NAME

BIRTHDAY

PHONE NUMBER

EMAIL ADDRESS

CONTACT METHOD

NOTES

NAME

BIRTHDAY

PHONE NUMBER

EMAIL ADDRESS

CONTACT METHOD

NOTES

NAME

BIRTHDAY

PHONE NUMBER

EMAIL ADDRESS

CONTACT METHOD

NOTES

NAME

BIRTHDAY

PHONE NUMBER

EMAIL ADDRESS

CONTACT METHOD

NOTES

NAME

BIRTHDAY

PHONE NUMBER

EMAIL ADDRESS

CONTACT METHOD

NOTES

NAME

BIRTHDAY

PHONE NUMBER

EMAIL ADDRESS

CONTACT METHOD

NOTES

NAME

BIRTHDAY

PHONE NUMBER

EMAIL ADDRESS

CONTACT METHOD

NOTES

NAME

BIRTHDAY

PHONE NUMBER

EMAIL ADDRESS

CONTACT METHOD

NOTES

NAME

BIRTHDAY

PHONE NUMBER

EMAIL ADDRESS

CONTACT METHOD

NOTES

NAME

BIRTHDAY

PHONE NUMBER

EMAIL ADDRESS

CONTACT METHOD

NOTES

attendance log

RUTH | A **SIMPLY BIBLE** STUDY

PARTICIPANT'S NAME	WEEK 1	WEEK 2	WEEK 3	WEEK 4	WEEK 5
1					
2					
3					
4					
5					
6					
7					
8					
9					
10					
11					
12					
13					
14					
15					

I AM THE VINE; YOU
ARE THE BRANCHES.
WHOEVER ABIDES IN ME
AND I IN HIM, HE IT IS
THAT BEARS MUCH FRUIT,
FOR APART FROM ME
YOU CAN DO NOTHING.

JOHN 15:5

prayer log

RUTH | A **SIMPLY BIBLE** STUDY

DATE	NAME	REQUEST	FOLLOW-UP

prayer log

RUTH | A **SIMPLY BIBLE** STUDY

DATE	NAME	REQUEST	FOLLOW-UP

prayer log

RUTH | A **SIMPLY BIBLE** STUDY

DATE	NAME	REQUEST	FOLLOW-UP

prayer log

DATE	NAME	REQUEST	FOLLOW-UP

prayer log

DATE	NAME	REQUEST	FOLLOW-UP

prayer log

RUTH | A **SIMPLY BIBLE** STUDY

DATE	NAME	REQUEST	FOLLOW-UP

AND WE KNOW THAT
FOR THOSE WHO LOVE GOD
ALL THINGS WORK TOGETHER
FOR GOOD, FOR THOSE WHO
ARE CALLED ACCORDING
TO HIS PURPOSE.

ROMANS 8:28

11237526R00085